I0426267

February 2012

MARITIME SECURITY

Coast Guard Needs to Improve Use and Management of Interagency Operations Centers

GAO

Accountability ★ Integrity ★ Reliability

GAO-12-202

February 2012

MARITIME SECURITY

Coast Guard Needs to Improve Use and Management of Interagency Operations Centers

Highlights of GAO-12-202, a report to congressional requesters

Why GAO Did This Study

The Coast Guard—a component of the Department of Homeland Security (DHS)—is responsible for establishing Interagency Operations Centers (IOC) in response to provisions of the Security and Accountability For Every (SAFE) Port Act of 2006. IOCs are designed to, among other things, share maritime information with the Coast Guard's port partners (other agencies and organizations it coordinates with). To facilitate IOCs, the Coast Guard is implementing an information-management and sharing system called WatchKeeper. GAO was asked to assess IOC and WatchKeeper implementation. This report addresses the extent to which (1) DHS and the Coast Guard have implemented IOCs, (2) port partners use WatchKeeper and the Coast Guard has facilitated its use to enhance IOC capabilities, and (3) the Coast Guard has adhered to established guidance in defining WatchKeeper requirements and its associated cost and schedule. GAO analyzed laws and documents, such as implementation plans, and interviewed Coast Guard and port-partner officials at the first four sectors (field locations) where WatchKeeper was implemented. The results of the four sector visits are not generalizable, but provide insights.

What GAO Recommends

GAO recommends that the Coast Guard collect data on port partners' access and use of WatchKeeper; develop, document, and implement a process on how to incorporate port-partner input; implement requirements-development practices; and revise the cost estimate and the integrated master schedule. DHS concurred subject to the availability of funds.

View GAO-12-202. For more information, contact Stephen L. Caldwell at (202) 512-9610 or caldwells@gao.gov.

What GAO Found

DHS and the Coast Guard did not meet the SAFE Port Act's requirement that IOCs be established at high-priority ports by October 2009, in part because the Coast Guard was not appropriated funds to establish the IOCs until 14 months after enactment of the law, and the definition of an IOC was evolving during this period. However, the Coast Guard plans to establish IOCs at all 35 of its sectors. According to the Coast Guard's analysis of sector status reports, none of its sectors have achieved IOCs with full operating capability. According to the Coast Guard's Chief of IOC Implementation, as well as its Information Sharing Executive Agent, continued support is needed from DHS to increase port-partner participation and the success of the IOC initiative. DHS has recently begun to support efforts to increase port-partner participation and further IOC implementation, such as facilitating the review of an IOC management directive. It is too early to determine, though, if and when IOCs will achieve their intended goal of sharing information and coordinating operations with port partners.

The Coast Guard has granted WatchKeeper access to port partners at 11 of the 12 sectors where it has been installed, but more than 80 percent of those port partners did not log on from July through September 2011. As of October 2011, the Coast Guard no longer collects data on port partners' access and use of WatchKeeper. Without such data, it will be difficult for the Coast Guard to determine whether WatchKeeper is facilitating the IOC program in meeting its goals of improving information sharing and coordination of joint operations. GAO interviewed 22 port partners who were not using WatchKeeper. Of those 22, the most frequently cited reason (by 7 port partners) is that it does not help them perform their missions. The Coast Guard primarily consulted with Customs and Border Protection when developing WatchKeeper, but did not solicit input from all port partners. Without developing, documenting, and implementing a process on how it will incorporate port partners' feedback into future WatchKeeper requirements, the Coast Guard does not have reasonable assurance that WatchKeeper will satisfy the needs of port partners and facilitate IOC goals.

The Coast Guard has not defined WatchKeeper requirements, cost, and schedule in accordance with established guidance. For example, the Coast Guard designed and developed the initial WatchKeeper segment without first defining the specific functions that the system is to perform. Further, the Coast Guard has not developed a reliable cost estimate to guide and inform the WatchKeeper investment. For example, the estimate does not include all government costs, such as related program-management costs. Also, WatchKeeper development and deployment has not been guided by a reliable schedule of the work needed to be performed and the key activities that need to occur. In particular, the schedule does not link all activities so that the project office can determine how a slip in a particular task may affect other related tasks, or the overall schedule. Project officials attributed these limitations to an aggressive IOC development schedule, limited resources, and competing priorities. As a result, these limitations increase the risk that WatchKeeper capabilities will not meet mission needs and will not be delivered on time and within budget.

_____ United States Government Accountability Office

Contents

Figures

Abbreviations

ATS	Automated Targeting System
CBP	U.S. Customs and Border Protection
CMMI®	Capability Maturity Model® Integration
DHS	Department of Homeland Security
FBI	Federal Bureau of Investigation
GIS	Geographic Information System
ICE	U.S. Immigration and Customs Enforcement
IM IPT	Information Management Integrated Project Team
IOC	Interagency Operations Center
ISGB	Information Sharing & Safeguarding Governance Board
JHOC	Joint Harbor Operations Center
JTTF	Joint Terrorism Task Force
MDA	maritime domain awareness
MUC	Maritime Unified Command
OFO	Office of Field Operations
SAFE Port Act	Security and Accountability For Every Port Act of 2006
SANS	Ship Arrival Notification System
SEI	Software Engineering Institute
WBS	work breakdown structure

United States Government Accountability Office
Washington, DC 20548

February 13, 2012

Congressional Requesters

To protect the nation's ports and waterways, the federal government strives to balance the need for mitigating security threats with minimizing disruption to the marine transportation system. Maritime security threats include the use of containerized cargo vessels to transport weapons of mass destruction; explosive-laden suicide boats as weapons; and vessels to smuggle people, drugs, weapons, and other contraband. To help secure the nation's marine transportation system against a potential terrorist attack or other harmful actions, maritime security stakeholders (port partners) seek to achieve maritime domain awareness (MDA)—the effective understanding of anything in the maritime environment that could affect the security, safety, economy, or environment of the United States.[1] The federal government has actively sought to enhance maritime security, but recognizes that no single department, agency, or entity holds all of the authorities and capabilities necessary to fully achieve effective MDA.

The Coast Guard, the lead Department of Homeland Security (DHS) component for MDA efforts, shares MDA information with federal, state, local, and tribal officials as an integral part of its efforts to secure the nation's marine transportation system against potential terrorist attacks. According to the Coast Guard's *Strategy for Maritime Safety, Security, and Stewardship*, the complexity and challenges of the maritime operating environment require that government agencies at all levels and stakeholders with maritime interests work together to achieve common objectives through increased coordination of efforts.[2] Specifically, the Coast Guard has ongoing partnerships with federal, state, and local law enforcement agencies. For example, at the federal level, the Coast Guard works with U.S. Customs and Border Protection (CBP) to: ensure that vessels arriving from overseas, their crews and passengers, and their

---

[1]Port partners include federal agencies and armed services such as U.S. Customs and Border Protection (CBP), U.S. Immigration and Custom Enforcement (ICE), and the U.S. Navy; state and local organizations such as port authorities, state law enforcement, and local law enforcement; and private-sector organizations such as marine exchanges.

[2]U.S. Coast Guard, *The U.S. Coast Guard Strategy for Maritime Safety, Security, and Stewardship* (Washington, D.C.: Jan. 19, 2007).

cargo are not security threats; and defend U.S. maritime borders against smugglers attempting to bring people, drugs, weapons, and other illegal contraband into the country. Further, at the state and local levels, the Coast Guard works with law enforcement agencies to, among other things, ensure the security of port operations and passenger ferries.

To increase its MDA capabilities, the Coast Guard is monitoring maritime activities, collecting intelligence, analyzing the threat environment, and sharing this information with port partners. One of these actions comes at least in part in response to provisions of the Security and Accountability For Every (SAFE) Port Act of 2006, which required the establishment of Interagency Operational Centers for port security to be incorporated in the implementation and administration of, among other things, maritime intelligence activities, information sharing, and short- and long-range vessel tracking.[3] In July 2007, the DHS Assistant Secretary for Legislative Affairs reported to Congress that the Coast Guard's acquisition project Command 21—originally named Command 2010, later named Command 21, and finally named the Interagency Operations Centers (IOC) project—would meet the Safe Port Act requirements for IOCs in 24 high-priority Coast Guard sectors.[4] The IOC project is, in part, designed to provide capabilities to increase MDA, automate data gathering, and provide decision support. Additionally, as originally designed, the IOC project was also to provide enhanced physical facilities and sensors to establish radar and camera coverage throughout ports. The IOC project also includes the development of an information management and sharing system, called WatchKeeper, that is to link information with operations to support situational awareness, joint planning, and mission execution. As the Coast Guard has moved ahead on the IOC project, it has established physical facilities for the colocation of port partners in some IOC locations. At these locations, WatchKeeper can be used to support the coordination that takes place among those agencies. The Coast Guard is also establishing IOC capabilities virtually—that is, sharing information and coordinating with port partners through an Internet web portal—and is

---

[3]Pub. L. No. 109-347, 120 Stat. 1884, 1892-93 (2006).

[4]Coast Guard sectors run all Coast Guard missions at the local and port level, such as search and rescue, port security, environmental protection, and law enforcement in ports and surrounding waters, and oversee a number of smaller Coast Guard units, including small cutters, small boat stations, and Aids to Navigation teams.

using WatchKeeper as an important information sharing tool to accomplish this.

You requested that we analyze the Coast Guard's management of the IOC concept and whether it properly integrates port partners' capabilities, concerns, and needs. As a result, this report addresses the following questions:

- To what extent have DHS and the Coast Guard implemented IOCs?

- To what extent are port partners using WatchKeeper and to what extent has the Coast Guard facilitated its use to enhance IOC capabilities?

- To what extent has the Coast Guard adhered to established guidance in defining WatchKeeper requirements and its associated cost and schedule?

To address the first objective, we analyzed pertinent provisions of the SAFE Port Act, as amended. We analyzed status reports provided by each of the 35 Coast Guard sectors and compared the Coast Guard's analysis of those status reports with the IOC requirements as defined in an internal Coast Guard message from the Assistant Commandant for Capability, and a draft annex to the *U.S. Coast Guard Sector Organization Manual*.[5] On the basis of our review of the sectors' status reports and interviews with the Coast Guard official who developed the criteria for the IOC requirements and analyzed the status reports, we determined the Coast Guard's analysis was reasonable to use for the purposes of our review. We interviewed Coast Guard officials in the Office of Shore Forces responsible for IOC requirements, as well as Coast Guard officials responsible for IOC implementation at their respective sector locations. We also conducted site visits to the five sectors where WatchKeeper was first implemented—Charleston, South Carolina; Hampton Roads, Virginia; Jacksonville, Florida; Detroit, Michigan; and San Diego, California. While the results of our site visits to these sectors cannot be generalized across all 35 Coast Guard sectors, we chose these locations to allow us to observe firsthand the status of IOC

---

[5]U.S. Coast Guard, *U.S. Coast Guard Sector Organization Manual*, COMDTINST M5401.6 (March 2008). The annex to this manual containing the IOC guidance is expected to be promulgated in January 2012.

implementation efforts. To evaluate the support DHS has provided to the Coast Guard for IOC implementation, we interviewed the Coast Guard's Chief of IOC Implementation and the Coast Guard's Information Sharing Executive Agent. We also interviewed officials from DHS's Information Sharing & Safeguarding Governance Board, the board providing support for IOC implementation. Further, we assessed DHS's involvement against criteria in the *Department of Homeland Security Information Sharing Strategy*,[6] which states that DHS should promote information sharing with federal partners.

To address the second objective, we used the Coast Guard's monthly log-on data to determine the number of port partners to whom the sectors provided WatchKeeper access and the extent to which these port partners accessed WatchKeeper. On the basis of our interviews with the Coast Guard officials responsible for the log-on data and review of responses provided by the Coast Guard's Research and Development Center on how the data are collected and maintained, we determined that the data from January 2011 through May 2011 were not reliable to determine the number of times port partners logged on to WatchKeeper since more log-ons were counted than should have been. However, we determined that the data were sufficiently reliable to use for interview selection of port partners who had or had not logged on. In contrast, we determined that the data from June 2011 through September 2011 were sufficiently reliable for the purposes of presenting the number of WatchKeeper users and respective number of WatchKeeper log-ons per month since the Coast Guard resolved the miscounting issue beginning with the June 2011 data.

Also, to address the second objective, we interviewed Coast Guard sector officials about the actions they took to increase their local port partners' use of WatchKeeper. We also interviewed 39 port partners at the first four sectors where WatchKeeper was implemented—Charleston, South Carolina; Hampton Roads, Virginia; Jacksonville, Florida; and Detroit, Michigan. We selected port partners to interview based on the Coast Guard's WatchKeeper log-on data from January 1, 2011—when the data were first collected—through March 31, 2011—the most recent data available at the time of the selection. At the four sectors, we requested

---

[6]DHS, *Department of Homeland Security Information Sharing Strategy* (Washington, D.C.: Apr. 18, 2008).

individual interviews with all port partners who had logged on to WatchKeeper to determine their perspectives on benefits derived from WatchKeeper, areas for improvement, if any, and the extent to which the Coast Guard has facilitated its use. In addition, we conducted focus groups and interviews with port partners who had been granted access to—but had not accessed—WatchKeeper to gather information on the reasons why they had not accessed WatchKeeper. To ensure the focus group participants represented each agency that had officials with access to WatchKeeper, we randomly selected participants within the four sectors, based on their agencies. While the results from our interviews and focus groups are not generalizable to all of the Coast Guard's port partners, they provided us accounts of how they perceived WatchKeeper's capabilities and potential benefits.

To determine the extent to which the Coast Guard solicited input from port partners during initial development of WatchKeeper, we analyzed documentation, including the *Interagency Operations Process Report: Mapping Process to Requirements for Interagency Operations Centers* and *Interagency Operations Centers Concept of Operations*,[7] and meeting minutes of sessions the Coast Guard held at select sectors, and discussed port partners' involvement with officials in the Office of Shore Forces responsible for IOC implementation. We assessed the Coast Guard's involvement of port partners against criteria in the *Department of Homeland Security Information Sharing Strategy*[8] and *Standards for Internal Control in the Federal Government*.[9] See appendix I for a list of port partners included in our individual interviews and focus groups at the sectors we visited.

To address the third objective, we analyzed relevant documentation, such as the IOC project *Operational Requirements Document*, the *Functional Requirements Document*, the *Systems Requirements Document*, the *Capability Development Plan*, and compared them to selected criteria from the Software Engineering Institute's (SEI) *Capability Maturity Model*®

---

[7]These documents are marked For Official Use Only and are not available to the public.

[8]DHS, *Department of Homeland Security Information Sharing Strategy* (April 2008).

[9]GAO, *Internal Control: Standards for Internal Control in the Federal Government*, GAO/AIMD-00-21.3.1 (Washington, D.C.: November 2009).

Integration for Acquisition,[10] to determine whether the Coast Guard fully defined requirements prior to designing, developing, testing, and deploying WatchKeeper; sufficiently prioritized WatchKeeper requirements; effectively managed requirements; and maintained traceability between operational requirements and system requirements. To determine the extent to which the Coast Guard had developed a reliable cost estimate for the IOC project, we evaluated the June 2010 life-cycle cost estimate relative to the four characteristics of a reliable estimate, as defined in GAO's *Cost Estimating and Assessment Guide.*[11] These four characteristics call for estimates to be comprehensive, well-documented, accurate, and credible, and the practices address, for example, the assumptions and source data used. We then characterized the extent to which each of the four characteristics was met as either Not Met, Partially Met, or Met.[12] To determine the extent to which the Coast Guard had developed a reliable schedule for the IOC project, we analyzed the IOC project integrated master schedule as of May 2011 because it was the most current schedule available at the time of our review, and we characterized our schedule findings into three categories: (1) comprehensive, (2) controlled, and (3) current.[13] Specifically, we analyzed the schedule against four of the key schedule estimating practices in GAO's *Cost Estimating and Assessment Guide* that represent the foundational elements of a reliable schedule.[14] In conducting our analysis, we used commercially available software tools to determine whether the schedule, for example, included all critical activities, a logical

---

[10]Software Engineering Institute (SEI), *Capability Maturity Model Integration (CMMI)*® *for Acquisition*, ver. 1.2 (Pittsburgh, Penn., November 2007).

[11]GAO, *GAO Cost Estimating and Assessment Guide: Best Practices for Developing and Managing Capital Program Costs*, GAO-09-3SP (Washington, D.C.: March 2009).

[12]"Not Met" = Coast Guard provided no evidence that satisfies any of the criterion. "Partially Met" = Coast Guard provided evidence that satisfies some, but not all, of the criterion.
"Met" = Coast Guard provided complete evidence that satisfies the entire criterion.

[13]Comprehensive is characterized as logically sequenced activities spanning the scope of work to be performed that are included in the schedule so that the full picture is available to managers. Controlled is characterized as the use of a documented process to manage changes to the schedule so that the integrity of the schedule is assured. Current is characterized as regularly updating ongoing activities using a formal process so that managers can readily know the status of the project.

[14]GAO-09-3SP.

sequence of activities, and a critical path.[15] Also, we interviewed project officials to determine the processes in place for developing, updating, maintaining, and controlling the schedule. For each area, we interviewed project officials to obtain clarification on the practices, and to determine the reasons for any deviations.

We conducted this performance audit from November 2010 to February 2012 in accordance with generally accepted government auditing standards. Those standards require that we plan and perform the audit to obtain sufficient, appropriate evidence to provide a reasonable basis for our findings and conclusions based on our audit objectives. We believe that the evidence obtained provides a reasonable basis for our findings and conclusions based on our audit objectives.

Background

Congress showed continuing interest in the development of IOCs shortly after the terrorist attacks of September 11, 2001. In the Consolidated Appropriations Resolution, 2003,[16] funding was appropriated specifically for such a center in Charleston, South Carolina. That center, known as Project SeaHawk, brought together agencies, including the Coast Guard, CBP, the Federal Bureau of Investigation (FBI), the Navy, and state and local law enforcement agencies, to improve transportation security. Shortly thereafter, the Coast Guard and Maritime Transportation Act of 2004[17] required the Commandant of the Coast Guard to report on the implementation and use of joint operational centers for security at certain United States ports.

The Coast Guard and the Navy also recognized the need to work together to ensure port security and developed local joint harbor operations centers (JHOC), which were to share information, improve awareness of port activities, and coordinate operations. These were originally created by local Coast Guard and Navy units, before the SAFE Port Act IOC requirement was enacted, to increase the security of naval vessels at their home ports. Later, in August 2005, the Coast Guard and

---

[15]The critical path represents the chain of dependent activities with the longest total duration in the schedule. If any activity on the critical path slips, the entire project will be delayed.

[16]Pub. L. No. 108-7, 117 Stat. 11, 53 (2003).

[17]Pub. L. No. 108-293, 118 Stat. 1028, 1082 (2004).

Navy signed a memorandum of agreement that officially established JHOCs to build upon the resources available to each service to produce better awareness of conditions and activities in ports with a large Navy presence. Eventually, JHOCs were established in Hampton Roads, Virginia; Jacksonville, Florida; San Diego, California; and Seattle, Washington. While these JHOCs were originally established as a means to improve information sharing and operational effectiveness between the Coast Guard and the Navy, other federal, state, and local port partners also began to operate within these centers. For example, CBP and the San Diego Harbor Patrol were also located in the San Diego JHOC.

In addition, the Bush administration expressed the need for port security stakeholders to work together. In particular, the National Strategy for Maritime Security, issued in September 2005, stated that agencies working to ensure maritime security should colocate in multiagency centers to facilitate direct interaction and efficient use of limited resources. Additionally, the strategy directed the agencies to develop well-defined coordination protocols and communication mechanisms for operating jointly.

Meanwhile, the Coast Guard began an initiative to help facilitate meeting its needs related to IOCs. In September 2005, the Coast Guard sent a request to DHS to authorize the initial phase of an acquisition project called Command 2010. Command 2010 was to improve the Coast Guard's capabilities for surveillance, decision and mission support, and multiagency collaboration. To improve the Coast Guard's surveillance capabilities in critical ports and coastal regions, Command 2010 was to provide a network of radar, cameras, and other sensors. To improve its decision and mission support capabilities, the Coast Guard planned to develop an information system—called WatchKeeper—that would provide situational awareness to Coast Guard personnel through displays of information gathered from sensors, as well as Coast Guard and port partner information sources. To improve collaboration, Command 2010 was also to include a web-based portal to allow port partners to access the same data displayed for the Coast Guard on WatchKeeper and allow joint access to Coast Guard and port partner operations schedules. The portal was to include collaboration functions, such as document management and message boards. Given these capabilities, Command 2010 was to support both IOCs where in-person coordination is possible and the virtual operations center concept as envisioned by the joint operations center working group. Virtual operations centers are in place when information sharing and operational coordination with port partners at separate locations occurs through the use of tools—in the case of

Command 2010, and as it evolved later to Command 21 and the IOC, on an Internet web portal.

Then, in 2006, the SAFE Port Act was enacted, which mandated that IOCs for port security be implemented at all high-priority ports within 3 years.[18] Under the SAFE Port Act, the Secretary of Homeland Security was to utilize, as appropriate, the characteristics of existing centers and provide for the participation, along with the Coast Guard, of other federal, state, local, and private-sector port security stakeholders, among other things.[19] Amendments to the IOC provisions in the Coast Guard Authorization Act of 2010 included adding that such centers should provide for the physical colocation of the Coast Guard and other stakeholders, where practicable.[20] Among other things, the 2010 act also required that the IOCs include information-management systems and sensor-management systems.

In June 2007, shortly after passage of the SAFE Port Act, the Coast Guard began a broader initiative to coordinate port-security efforts. Specifically, CBP and the Coast Guard formed a joint operations center working group that was to improve near- and long-term efficiency and effectiveness of joint field operations. The working group visited select Coast Guard and CBP field units to gather firsthand knowledge of Coast Guard and CBP working relationships. According to the working group, the site visits revealed interagency coordination was already occurring in ways deemed most appropriate by local field commanders. Also, the working group conducted a survey of Coast Guard and CBP field commanders that highlighted, among other things, that in-person collaboration is desirable for more-effective Coast Guard and CBP relations, but that virtual operations centers should be considered when in-person coordination was not feasible.

---

[18]The SAFE Port Act did not define the term "high-priority ports," but in response to a reporting requirement included in the act, DHS stated that its list of priority ports was based on factors including risk-assessment scores, port-criticality ratings, Department of Defense and Department of Justice partnership priorities, and business factors such as investments in facilities and sensors.

[19]The SAFE Port Act named pilot IOCs in Miami, Florida; Norfolk/Hampton Roads, Virginia; Charleston, South Carolina; and San Diego, California; and a virtual operation center at the Port of New York and New Jersey. Subsequent amendments to the IOC statutory provisions deleted the specific listing of these particular IOCs.

[20]Pub. L. No. 111-281, 124 Stat. 2905, 2990 (2010).

The Coast Guard received $60 million of funding that Congress directed to the IOC project in annual fiscal year 2008 appropriations to begin the process of establishing IOCs.[21] The Coast Guard received an additional $14 million in congressionally directed appropriations from fiscal years 2009 through 2012 for IOC implementation.[22]

Coast Guard Did Not Meet the Required Deadline for Establishing IOCs, but Has Made Progress

The Coast Guard did not meet the October 2009 deadline enacted in the SAFE Port Act to establish IOCs; however, the Coast Guard is establishing IOCs at all 35 of its sectors, although none of them have achieved full operating capability. According to the Coast Guard's Chief of IOC Implementation and its Information Sharing Executive Agent, continued support is needed from DHS to increase port-partner participation and the success of the IOC initiative. DHS has recently begun to support efforts to increase port-partner participation and further IOC implementation.

Coast Guard Did Not Meet the SAFE Port Act IOC Deadline, and Its Definition of an IOC Has Evolved

The Coast Guard did not meet the SAFE Port Act's deadline to establish IOCs at high-risk ports within 3 years of enactment, in part because it was not appropriated funds to establish the IOCs until fiscal year 2008—14 months after enactment of the law, and because the definition of a fully operational IOC was evolving during this period. According to the Coast Guard, unexpected and unreliable funding sources created the challenge in scheduling and meeting planned milestones as each change required cost and schedule adjustments. However, funding was provided nearly 2 years before the required deadline, and in our analysis of the Coast Guard's actions leading up to the deadline, development of the IOCs was not prioritized until the deadline passed. The Coast Guard made several

---

[21]H. Comm. on Appropriations, 110th Cong., Committee Print on H.R. 2764 / Public Law 110-161, Division E – Department of Homeland Security Appropriations Act, 2008, at 1060-62 (2007), accompanying the Consolidated Appropriations Act, 2008 (Pub. L. No. 110-161, 121 Stat. 2042 [2007]).

[22]H. Comm. on Appropriations, 110th Cong., Committee Print on H.R. 2638 / Public Law 110-329, Division D – Department of Homeland Security Appropriations Act, 2009, at 647 (2008), accompanying the Consolidated Security, Disaster Assistance, and Continuing Appropriations Act, 2009 (Pub. L. No. 110-329, 122 Stat. 3574 (2008)); H. R. Conf. Rep. No. 111-298, at 86-90 (2009), accompanying the Department of Homeland Security Appropriations Act, 2010 (Pub. L. No. 111-83, 123 Stat. 2142 (2009)); H. R. Conf. Rep. No. 112-331, at 979 (2011), accompanying the Consolidated Appropriations Act, 2012 (Pub. L. No. 112-74, 125 Stat. 786 (2011)).

changes to its efforts to develop IOCs from 2007 through 2009. For example, in its July 2007 letter to Congress on the budget and cost-sharing analysis of implementing the IOC requirements of the SAFE Port Act, DHS reported changing the name of the project—from Command 2010 to Command 21. In this letter, the DHS Assistant Secretary for Legislative Affairs stated that Command 21 was the Coast Guard acquisition project that was to provide the IOC capability required by the SAFE Port Act. This acquisition project was to provide information-management tools to improve interagency coordination, enhance awareness, and automate anomaly detection. Command 21 was to accomplish these tasks by facilitating interagency cooperation, information sharing, and joint, port-level operations through the use of WatchKeeper; as well as providing a sensor network and facility upgrades to facilitate multiagency operations and provide space for port partners. Figure 1 depicts the type of information that WatchKeeper provides to the Coast Guard and port partners.

Figure 1: Information WatchKeeper Provides to the Coast Guard and Port Partners

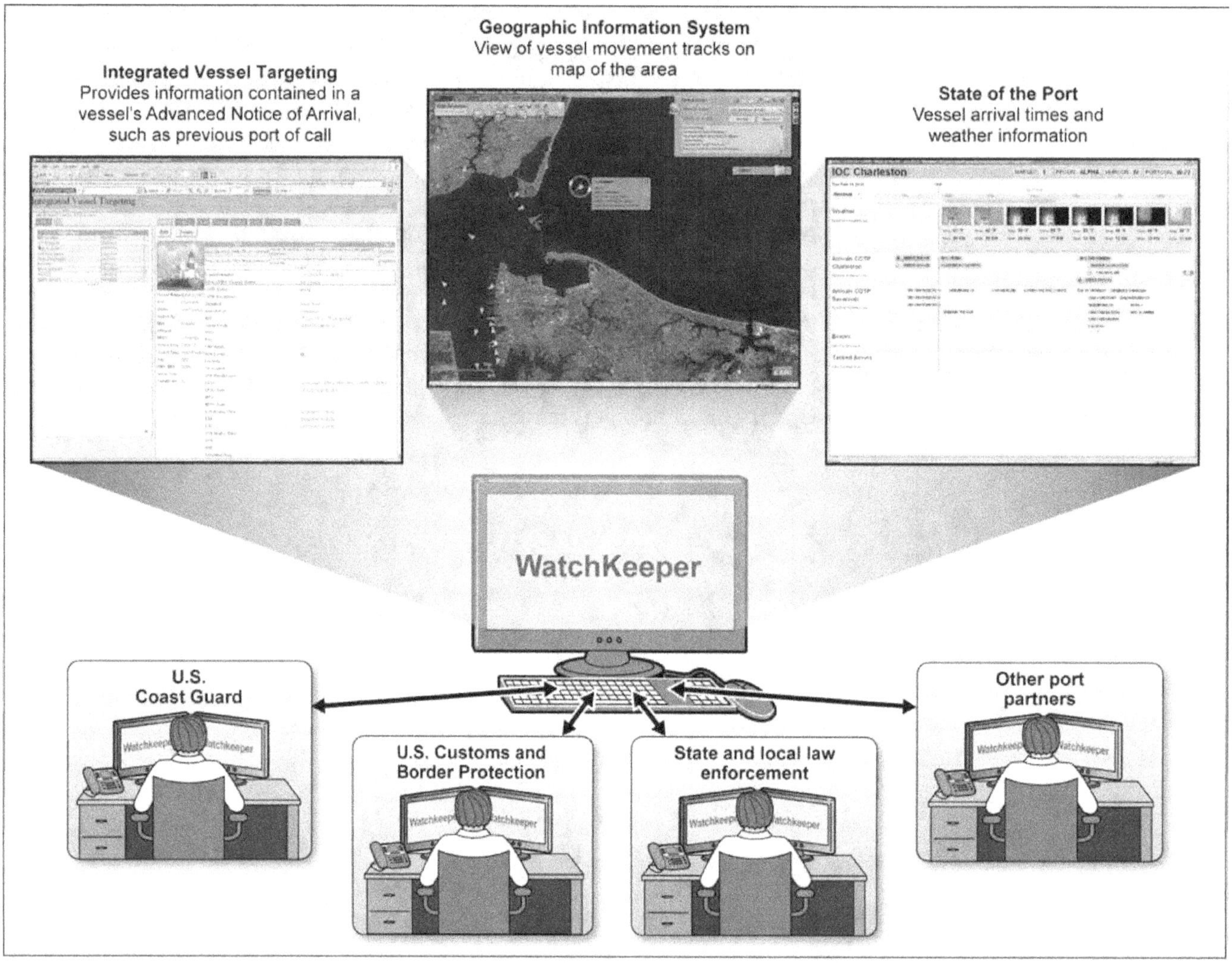

Source: GAO analysis of Coast Guard information.

In March 2008, the Coast Guard reported that physical colocation with port partners was preferred, but interagency coordination and cooperation would also occur virtually. These virtual interactions would be facilitated by sharing information through WatchKeeper. However, 36 of 39 port partners we spoke with expressed views on physical and virtual colocation, and 31 of those 36 port partners expressed benefits to being colocated with the Coast Guard. For example, one port partner working at the IOC in Charleston, South Carolina, stated that sharing space with the Coast Guard allows for easier communication with Coast Guard officials because they are just down the hall. He also said that the Coast Guard's policy of rotating officials every 3 years could hinder the success of virtual IOCs because relationships with the local Coast Guard representatives will not have been established. Another port partner we spoke with said that the virtual IOC in Hampton Roads, Virginia, has been effective because there are weekly in-person meetings that allow trust to be built, which facilitates the virtual meetings conducted using WatchKeeper. While there are clearly disadvantages to not being colocated, Coast Guard officials stated that funding levels prevented it from pursuing physical IOCs beyond locations in San Francisco, California; New Orleans, Louisiana; and Wilmington, North Carolina.

The Coast Guard communicated changes to Command 21 in a 2008 letter to congressional appropriations committees. In the letter, the Coast Guard Commandant further refined the implementation of Coast Guard efforts to meet its IOC mandate. In particular, he stated that the Coast Guard planned to install the WatchKeeper information-management tools, the sensor network, and facility upgrades at the 24 Coast Guard sectors that encompassed the nation's high-priority ports. All 35 sectors would, at a minimum, receive WatchKeeper. Additionally, user feedback based on the initial installations would be used as a guide to finalize requirements. Also in 2008, the IOC plans changed from having a separate collaboration portal to share information on WatchKeeper with port partners to building that communications mechanism as a part of WatchKeeper.

In August 2009, the Coast Guard established four implementation segments for what it was now calling the IOC/Command 21 project.[23] At that time, the segments were:

- **Segment 1**: Provide a standardized information-management solution (WatchKeeper) focused on integrated vessel targeting, operations planning, and operations monitoring and interoperability.

- **Segment 2**: Provide integrated sensor management with linkages to existing sensors.

---

[23]By October 2009, the Coast Guard began calling the acquisition project the Interagency Operations Centers project—or IOC project.

GAO-12-202 Maritime Domain Awareness

- **Segment 3**: Provide expanded sensors to fill gaps in situational awareness.

- **Segment 4**: Upgrade existing facilities to support interagency planning and operations, including space allocation for key port partners.

While these actions represented the initial planning steps of developing the IOCs, the Coast Guard did not provide sector commanding officers with guidance on the required elements for an IOC until March 2010, 5 months after the deadline to establish the IOCs. Coast Guard officials stated that this was because the initial focus was on the acquisition of WatchKeeper and not the IOC initiative as a whole. In March 2010, the Assistant Commandant of Capability sent a message to the sectors outlining the five elements an IOC needs to function optimally. Described below, these five elements constitute the Coast Guard's definition of a fully operational IOC.

1. Clearly defined governance and membership, including documented agreements regarding which agencies will participate, in which ways, where, and when.

2. Joint, coordinated operational activities (e.g., inspections, vessel boardings, patrols, and exercises) as appropriate.

3. Shared visibility of the operational schedules of maritime assets and known events.

4. A regular schedule of coordination meetings with federal, state, and local port partner representatives from each member agency.

5. Shared access to interagency information-management systems (e.g., WatchKeeper) where they are in place.

The Majority of Sectors' IOCs Have Achieved Initial Operating Capability; Prior Collaboration Is a Key Determinant of IOC Progress

As of October 2010, 32 of the 35 sectors had made progress in implementing IOCs, but none of the IOCs had achieved full operating capability.[24] According to the Coast Guard, the sectors expressed concern that when they provided the information to Coast Guard headquarters in October 2010, they were unaware of how their progress would be measured and, therefore, omitted pertinent information on actions that meet the five IOC elements. The Coast Guard plans to reevaluate the sectors' progress in 2012. The Coast Guard analyzed the sectors' October 2010 status reports using criteria it developed for each of the five required IOC elements previously discussed. Specifically, each sector was assigned points on a scale of 1 to 100 in terms of the progress it has made toward meeting the criteria associated with the first four IOC elements (all except WatchKeeper), with 100 being the highest. Each sector was then placed in one of the following categories based on the average number of points it received for the first four IOC elements:

- **initial operating capability**: sectors that have met 30 to less than 55 percent of the criteria;

- **initial-advanced operating capability**: sectors that have met 55 to less than 80 percent of the criteria; or

- **final operating capability**: sectors that have met 80 percent or more of the criteria.

According to the Coast Guard's analysis of the 35 sectors, as of October 2010, 3 have not achieved initial operating capability for their IOCs, 22 had achieved IOC initial operating capability, 10 had achieved IOC initial-advanced operating capability, and none had achieved IOC full operating capability. Of the 10 Coast Guard sectors that have achieved IOC initial-advanced operating capability, 5 were recognized by the Coast Guard in 2008 as sectors with a high degree of collaboration with port partners. In particular, these sectors had established a means to coordinate with their port partners prior to the Coast Guard developing the five IOC elements, and in some cases prior to the October 2006 enactment of the SAFE Port Act IOC requirements. For example, during our site visit to Coast Guard Sector San Diego—the sector that had made the greatest progress in meeting the IOC requirements—we observed port partners coordinating

---

[24]The September 2010 request is the most recent request the Coast Guard has made to its sectors to determine their progress in implementing IOCs.

joint operations during one of the Maritime Unified Command's (MUC) weekly meetings. The MUC is an alliance of federal, state, and local law enforcement agencies that addresses threats in San Diego's maritime domain, such as drug and alien smuggling. We also observed the JHOC where MUC members can coordinate joint operations and exchange information. Figure 2 below depicts the IOC implementation status of each of the 35 Coast Guard sectors.

Figure 2: IOC Implementation Status by Sector

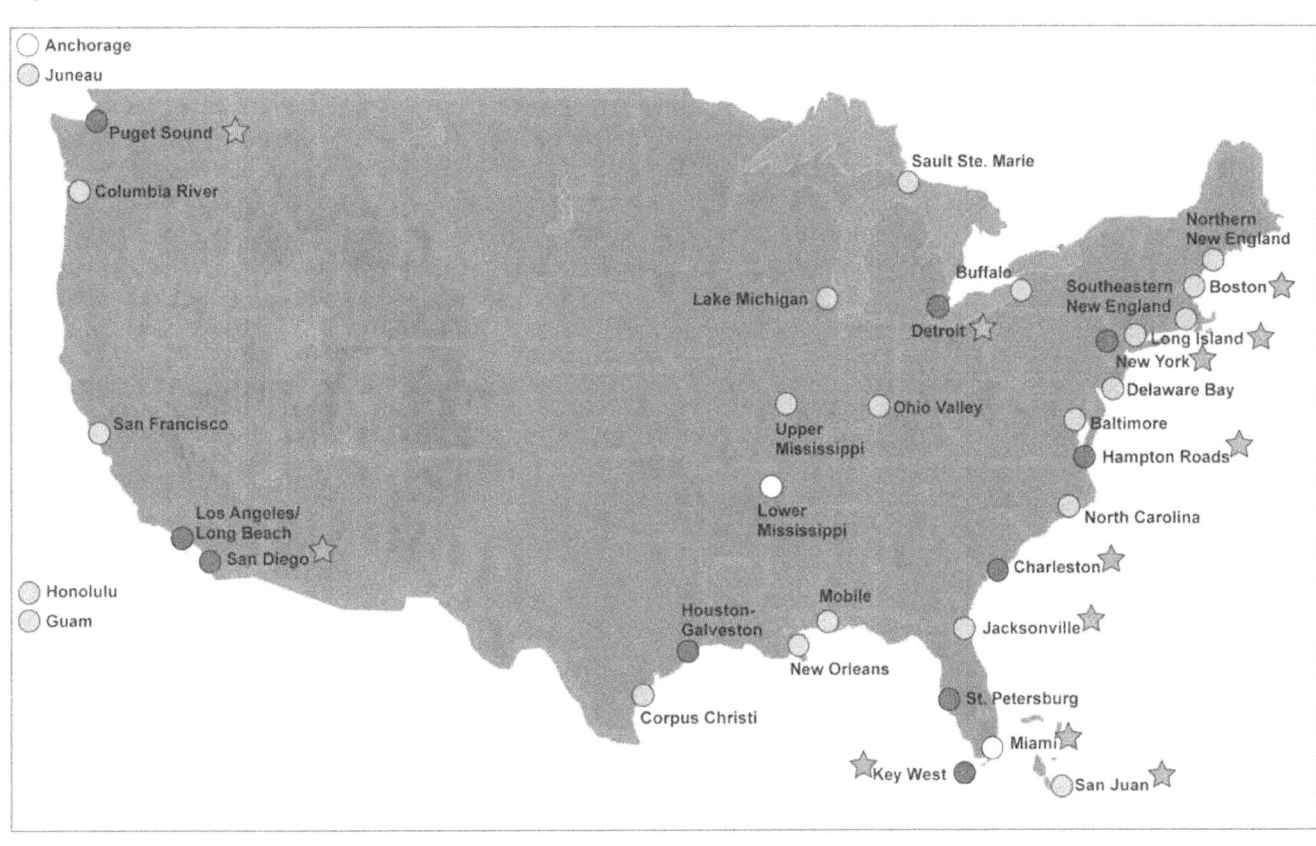

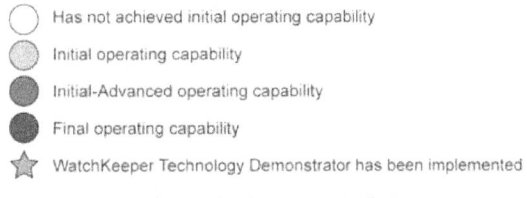

Source: GAO using U.S. Coast Guard data (data); Map Explosion (map)

Note: WatchKeeper implementation is as of September 2011. IOC implementation status is as of October 2010, at which time no sector had achieved final operating capability.

The results of the Coast Guard analysis of the first four IOC elements indicate that sectors have made the greatest progress in achieving regularly scheduled coordination meetings (element 4), followed closely by joint coordinated operations (element 2), and shared visibility of schedule and assets (element 3). The sectors have made the least progress in clearly defining IOC governance (element 1), with sectors, on average, achieving 29 percent of this criteria. Figure 3 depicts the progress the sectors have made, by element, based on the average of the individual sector percentages.

The fifth IOC element involves sectors utilizing and providing their port partners access to WatchKeeper. The extent of capabilities that WatchKeeper provides the sectors is not part of the Coast Guard's measure of IOC implementation. Since sectors are unable to control when WatchKeeper will be implemented at their respective locations, the Coast Guard is analyzing the sectors' progress in meeting this element separately from the other four IOC elements.

Figure 3: Average Percentage of IOC Implementation across Coast Guard Sectors, for Four of the Five IOC Elements, as of October 2010

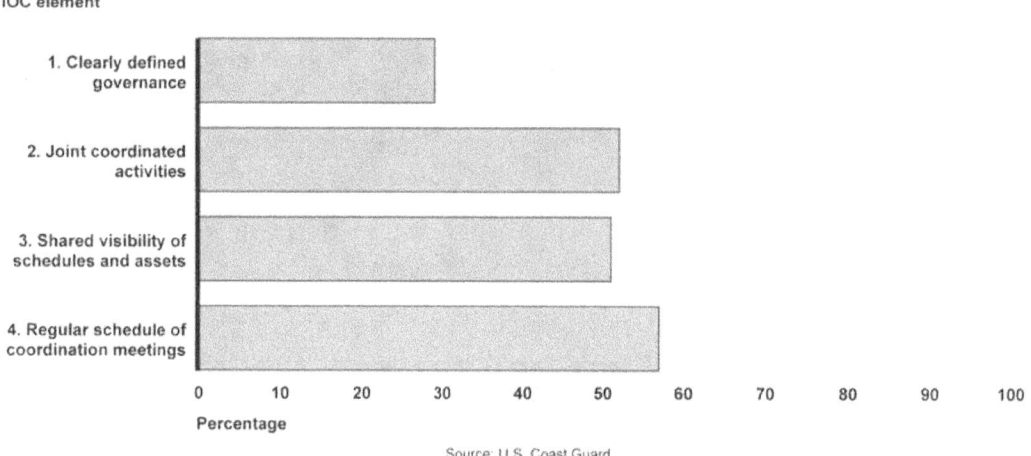

IOC element

Percentage

Source: U.S. Coast Guard

In September 2009, the Coast Guard released initial WatchKeeper capabilities to Sector Charleston, South Carolina. However, in March 2010, an operational test and evaluation revealed limitations in the maturity of the technology. As a result, the Coast Guard halted further deployment of WatchKeeper to additional IOC locations. In May 2010, DHS authorized the IOC project to release WatchKeeper as a technology demonstrator to all 35 IOC locations.[25] By August 2010, the Coast Guard stated that Segment 1 of the IOC project—made up of the WatchKeeper Technology Demonstrator—would initially be released to 17 sectors, and then to the remaining 18 if there was a positive cost-benefit to doing so. As of September 2011, the WatchKeeper Technology Demonstrator has been implemented at 12 sectors (see fig. 2 above). The Coast Guard anticipates that it will implement the WatchKeeper Technology Demonstrator at five more sectors by April 2012. According to the Coast Guard's Acquisition Program Baseline, implementing WatchKeeper at the remaining 18 sectors is to be complete by March 2017. As sectors receive WatchKeeper, the Coast Guard plans to measure their progress based on the extent to which they are both utilizing WatchKeeper and providing access to port partners. As of September 2011, the first two sectors to receive the WatchKeeper Technology Demonstrator—Charleston, South Carolina, and Hampton Roads, Virginia—granted the greatest number of port partners access to WatchKeeper (53 and 62 respectively). The port partners granted access by these sectors include officials from federal, state, and local agencies.

The Coast Guard IOC Project Manager stated that the Coast Guard does not expect to proceed with Segments 3 and 4 of the IOC project—the addition of new sensors and building new facilities—beyond the planning proposals for five sectors and the construction at three locations because of funding uncertainties.[26]

DHS Has Recently Begun to Support Port-Partner Participation and Further IOC Implementation

According to the Coast Guard's Chief of IOC Implementation and its Information Sharing Executive Agent, continued support is needed from DHS to increase port-partner participation and the success of the IOC initiative. The SAFE Port Act IOC provision does not compel port partners to participate in IOCs, so although DHS delegated authority for IOC implementation to the Coast Guard, it cannot implement IOCs in isolation. According to the Coast Guard's Chief of IOC Implementation, DHS agencies developed an IOC Concept of Operations in 2006, but the effort

---

[25]A technology demonstrator can be used to define requirements, verify system designs, evaluate technology maturity, or support deployment decisions.

[26]The design and survey work was performed at Sectors Detroit, Honolulu, Lake Michigan, Mobile, and St. Petersburg. The construction, reconfiguration, or outfitting was performed at Sectors New Orleans, San Francisco, and Wilmington.

GAO-12-202 Maritime Domain Awareness

floundered since other DHS agencies were not willing to sign the agreement. According to Coast Guard officials, once DHS delegated responsibility for the development of IOCs to the Coast Guard, the department did not provide any support or guidance on how to implement IOCs. According to a DHS Information Sharing & Safeguarding Governance Board (ISGB) official, the ISGB was not aware the Coast Guard needed support until mid-2011.

In July 2011, the Coast Guard requested that the ISGB adopt the IOC initiative as an information-sharing priority initiative. The ISGB approved this request and directed the board members to assist in formulating information-sharing and access policy and standardized procedures for IOCs, through a DHS IOC Integrated Process Team with representation from all DHS offices and components who have experience specific to information sharing with non-DHS partners. According to Coast Guard and ISGB officials, in August 2011, the ISGB solicited comments on a draft management directive authored by the Coast Guard to instruct DHS agencies to participate in IOCs. The directive was issued in December 2011.

While the Coast Guard and DHS are working to increase participation at IOCs, the Coast Guard has experienced challenges in maintaining port-partner participation at its physical IOC locations. According to ISGB officials, obtaining DHS support for IOCs is a first step in building IOC participation. Subsequent steps involve obtaining support from non-DHS federal agencies, as well as state and local agencies. The experience to date with non-DHS agency involvement at current IOCs has been mixed. For example, the Navy, which was a partner at the JHOCs, has withdrawn its watchstanders from these locations. In at least one JHOC location (Jacksonville, Florida), the Coast Guard also lost the use of the facility that was used as the JHOC, as well as access to the Navy's sensor network. Coast Guard officials told us that these events occurred due to funding constraints and other priorities. In contrast, in at least one other JHOC location (Hampton Roads, Virginia), the Navy is working with the Coast Guard sector there to develop and implement a full scale IOC. Similarly, while the Joint Terrorism Task Force left the SeaHawk facility in Charleston, South Carolina, when funding for SeaHawk was moved from the Department of Justice to the Coast Guard, the task force maintains a representative at the facility. The ISGB plans to assist the Coast Guard with establishing information-sharing agreements with state and local agencies and utilizing the White House–based Information Sharing and Access Interagency Policy Committee as a mechanism for obtaining support from non-DHS federal agencies. However, it is too early to determine how successful these efforts will be in facilitating the IOC's role in sharing critical information among port partners.

WatchKeeper Is Not Being Used by Majority of Port Partners; Monitoring Participation and Soliciting Input Could Help Improve System

The Coast Guard has granted WatchKeeper access to port partners at 11 of the 12 sectors where it has been installed, but the majority of those port partners with access were not using the system frequently, with more than 80 percent of port partners not logging on to the system from July through September 2011. Port partners have expressed mixed views on the usefulness of WatchKeeper and would like to see additional features and information incorporated to enhance its capabilities. The Coast Guard has recently taken action to increase WatchKeeper log ons by its port partners, but could do more to obtain input on port partners' needs in order to increase their WatchKeeper use.

More Than 80 Percent of Port Partners Are Not Logging On to WatchKeeper, and Coast Guard No Longer Has an Approach for Systematically Monitoring System Use

Port Partners' Use of WatchKeeper

Coast Guard sectors granted WatchKeeper access to 233 port partners as of September 2011, as shown in table 1. However, most of these port partners were not logging on.

Table 1: Number of Port Partners with WatchKeeper Access by Sector, as of September 2011

Coast Guard sector	WatchKeeper installation date	Number of port partners
Charleston	February 2010	53
Hampton Roads	June 2010	62
Jacksonville	September 2010	19
Detroit	October 2010	31
San Diego	January 2011	4
Puget Sound	February 2011	28
New York	March 2011	14
Long Island Sound	May 2011	1
Boston	June 2011	5
Miami	July 2011	12
Key West	July 2011	4
San Juan	August 2011	0
Total		**233**

Source: GAO using information provided by the U.S. Coast Guard.

Our analysis of WatchKeeper log-on data shows that of the 233 port partners who had access to WatchKeeper for any part of September 2011 (the most recent month for which data were available), 192 (about 82 percent) did not log on to the system, 35 (about 15 percent) logged on between 1 to 5 times, and 6 (about 3 percent) logged on more than 5 times.[27] Figure 4 depicts the number of port partners who logged on during the month of September 2011.

---

[27]Since port partners have no opportunity to log on to WatchKeeper until after access is granted, those who are granted access late in a month may, therefore, not have an opportunity to log on until the following month.

Figure 4: Number of Port Partners Logging On to WatchKeeper during September 2011

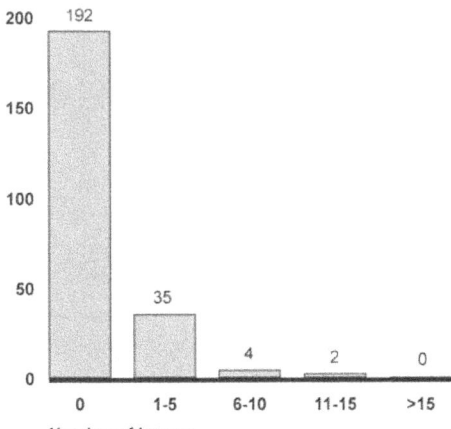

Source: GAO analysis of U.S. Coast Guard data.

Although Coast Guard officials have increased the number of port partners with access to WatchKeeper across its sectors, a gap remains between those with access and those logging on to WatchKeeper, as shown in figure 5. For example, from June through September 2011, the Coast Guard added from 6 to 26 new users each month, but the percentage of users with access who logged on to WatchKeeper remained at 18 percent for July through September 2011.

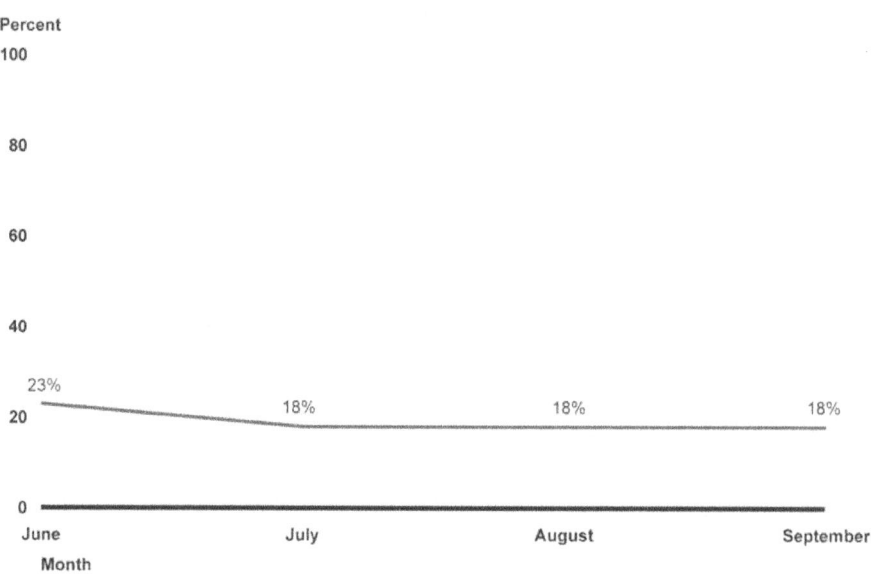

Figure 5: Percentage of Port Partners Logging On to WatchKeeper, June through September 2011

Percent

Source: GAO analysis of U.S. Coast Guard data.

The Coast Guard IOC Project Manager entered into an internal contract with the Research and Development Center to measure and report monthly on the number of WatchKeeper accounts held and log ons to the system by the Coast Guard and port partners. The first report was issued related to activity occurring during January 2011 and continued to be issued monthly through September 2011. After the September report was issued, the contract expired and as of November 2011, the Coast Guard has not determined whether it will enter into any future contracts to collect similar data. Therefore, the Coast Guard no longer has an approach in place for systematically monitoring port partners' use of WatchKeeper. Leading federal practices for performance management require federal agencies to (1) measure progress toward achieving their goals, (2) identify which external factors might affect such progress, and (3) explain why a goal was not met.[28] Without a means to determine to what extent (1) sectors are providing port partners WatchKeeper access and (2) port

---

[28]GAO, *Program Evaluation: Studies Helped Agencies Measure or Explain Program Performance*, GAO/GGD-00-204 (Washington, D.C.: Sept. 29, 2000).

GAO-12-202 Maritime Domain Awareness

partners are using WatchKeeper, it will be difficult for the Coast Guard to determine whether WatchKeeper is facilitating the IOC initiative in meeting its goals of improving information sharing and coordination of joint operations.

Port Partners' Views of WatchKeeper

Most of the 39 port partners we interviewed expressed mixed views on the usefulness of WatchKeeper and provided examples of other features and information that they would like to see incorporated to enhance its capabilities.[29] We interviewed 17 port partners who used WatchKeeper, and they provided us with a variety of reasons for why they are using WatchKeeper. Among them, 8 port partners stated that they use WatchKeeper to obtain information on vessels—such as which port a vessel is coming from or arriving at—to perform their own missions; 8 port partners stated that they use WatchKeeper features—such as the Geographic Information System (GIS)[30]—to perform their own missions; and 5 port partners said they use WatchKeeper as a tool to facilitate coordination with the Coast Guard during vessel targeting meetings. See appendix II for more information on port-partner views about reasons they use the system.

Although 17 of the 39 port partners we spoke with are using WatchKeeper, 21 port partners provided us with a variety of reasons as to why they are not using WatchKeeper.[31] Among them, 7 port partners stated that WatchKeeper does not help them perform their own missions; 5 stated that they are able to obtain and share information with Coast Guard officials in-person; and 5 port partners said that they are not able to access all features of WatchKeeper because of a firewall. See appendix II for more information on port partners' responses.

Port partners we interviewed provided examples of other features and information that they would like to see incorporated into WatchKeeper to

---

[29]A total of 39 port partners with access to WatchKeeper at sectors agreed to participate in interviews and focus groups with us. See app. I for a list of the port partners we interviewed.

[30]GIS displays a ship's locations based on its automatic identification system, which is a maritime digital-communication system that continually transmits and receives vessel data over very-high frequencies to identify and track vessels.

[31]A total of 22 port partners we interviewed are not using WatchKeeper. One port partner did not provide a reason why not.

GAO-12-202 Maritime Domain Awareness

enhance its capabilities and, thus, increase the benefits of WatchKeeper to users other than the Coast Guard. Specifically, of the 39 port partners we interviewed, 19 provided us feedback on the features or information they would like added to WatchKeeper. Adding crew and passenger information, which is contained in the Coast Guard's Ship Arrival Notification System (SANS),[32] was the most requested, with 8 of the 19 port partners desiring this information. The second-most-requested information and features, each cited by 4 port partners, was the inclusion of information from CBP's Automated Targeting System (ATS),[33] and the inclusion of sensors.

Coast Guard Has Taken Action to Increase Port Partners' Use of WatchKeeper, but Could Enhance WatchKeeper Use by Soliciting More Port-Partner Input

The Coast Guard has recently taken steps to increase port partners' use of WatchKeeper. For example, the Coast Guard has offered port partners training on WatchKeeper. Of the 39 port partners we interviewed with access to WatchKeeper, 35 reported that they had been offered training by the Coast Guard. In addition, the Coast Guard established an information-technology help desk that WatchKeeper users can call or e-mail for support, which has assisted port partners. Further, during the course of our review, in June 2011, the Coast Guard began reaching out to its port partners by means of an online survey to obtain feedback on their use of WatchKeeper and to solicit information on areas for improvement. The Coast Guard has also taken actions to increase the information available to port partners through WatchKeeper. According to Coast Guard officials, they are aware that port partners want access to crew and passenger information through WatchKeeper and they are developing different levels of access rights to allow for certain port partners to have access to such information while limiting the access to

[32]The SANS database is populated with Notice of Arrival information provided by vessels 96 hours prior to entering U.S. territorial waters. Coast Guard Command Centers can access this database to gather vessel, crew, cargo, and company information concerning ships entering their area of responsibility.

[33]CBP uses ATS—a mathematical model that uses weighted rules to assign a risk score to arriving cargo shipments based on shipping information—to help identify and prevent potential terrorists and terrorist weapons from entering the United States. ATS is used by CBP to review documentation, including cargo manifest information submitted by the vessel carriers on all U.S.-bound shipments, and entry data (more detailed information about the cargo) submitted by brokers, to develop risk scores that help identify containers for additional examination.

others.[34] Additionally, in May 2011, the Coast Guard and CBP—a port-partner agency—agreed that exchanging information would be beneficial to both agencies. In a July 2011 memo, the Coast Guard IOC Project Manager identified certain information (e.g., hazardous cargo manifests) from CBP's ATS to include in WatchKeeper. In October 2011, CBP and Coast Guard officials met to plan the information exchange, estimated to occur in May 2012.

According to the Coast Guard, it consulted with CBP and U.S. Immigration and Customs Enforcement (ICE) when developing the initial requirements for WatchKeeper. However, the Coast Guard did not solicit input from all port partners prior to developing requirements for WatchKeeper. For example, our review of meeting minutes from site visits conducted by an IOC working group to Sectors Jacksonville and New Orleans indicate that CBP officials were present in Jacksonville and CBP, ICE, port, local emergency-preparedness, state police, and harbor police officials were present in New Orleans, but the Coast Guard did not solicit input from these other port partners.[35] According to Coast Guard officials, port partner involvement in the development of WatchKeeper requirements was primarily limited to CBP because WatchKeeper grew out of a system designed for screening commercial vessel arrivals, which is a CBP mission. However, according to the *Interagency Operations Process Report: Mapping Process to Requirements for Interagency Operations Centers*, the Coast Guard identified many port partners as critical to IOCs, including other federal agencies (e.g., the Federal Bureau of Investigation) and state and local agencies.[36] Moreover, the *Department of Homeland Security Information Sharing Strategy* states that DHS shall "ensure that DHS technology platforms evolve to facilitate appropriate mission-based information sharing with Federal, State, local, territorial, tribal, private sector and foreign partners."[37] In addition, GAO's *Standards for Internal Control in the Federal Government* state that, "management should ensure there are adequate means of

---

[34]These changes are being made to reflect differences among port partners' authority to receive personally identifiable information.

[35]The IOC working group also conducted a site visit to Sector New York, but the Coast Guard was unable to locate the meeting minutes from this visit.

[36]This document is not available to the public.

[37]DHS, *Department of Homeland Security Information Sharing Strategy* (April 2008).

communicating with and obtaining information from external stakeholders that may have a significant impact on the agency achieving its goals."[38] The Coast Guard has identified port-partner participation as important to a successful IOC, recognizing that without it, there will highly likely be a significant consequence to the success of the IOC initiative. Without a process to obtain and incorporate port-partner input into the development of future WatchKeeper requirements, the Coast Guard does not have reasonable assurance that WatchKeeper will satisfy port partners' needs, and facilitate mission-based information sharing to achieve the goals of the IOC project.

Coast Guard Has Not Adhered to Established Guidance in Defining WatchKeeper Requirements, Cost, and Schedule

The Coast Guard has not adhered to established guidance in defining WatchKeeper requirements, cost, and schedule, which are fundamental to delivering a system on time and within budget. In particular, the Coast Guard has not (1) effectively developed and managed WatchKeeper requirements, (2) developed a reliable cost estimate to guide and inform the WatchKeeper investment, and (3) developed a reliable project schedule to develop and deploy WatchKeeper.

Coast Guard Has Not Effectively Developed and Managed WatchKeeper Requirements

Well-defined and managed requirements are a cornerstone of effective system development and acquisition. According to the Software Engineering Institute's (SEI) *Capability Maturity Model® Integration* (CMMI®) *for Acquisition*, effective requirements development and management include, among other things, (1) developing and documenting requirements before initiating design and development; (2) prioritizing requirements to ensure that those most critical to stakeholders and users are addressed early; and (3) ensuring forward and backward traceability between higher-level business requirements and more-detailed system requirements.[39]

The Coast Guard has not implemented these three aspects of effective requirements development and management. First, the Coast Guard did

---

[38]GAO/AIMD-00-21.3.1.

[39]SEI, *CMMI® for Acquisition.*

not fully define requirements prior to designing, developing, testing, and deploying WatchKeeper. Recognized guidance calls for first defining business requirements that describe how users will interact with the system, and user needs in terms of what the system is to do and how it is to do it, to ensure that the developed system satisfies user needs.[40] Although the Coast Guard developed draft high-level business requirements for WatchKeeper, it did not define the specific functions that the system is to perform, and as noted above, it did not elicit input from all port partners in developing the high-level requirements. Coast Guard officials acknowledged that they should have developed requirements before designing and developing WatchKeeper, but stated that there was not enough time between receiving project funding in fiscal year 2008 and the SAFE Port Act's deadline to establish the IOCs (and its information-management and sharing system—WatchKeeper) in 2009. The lack of well-defined business requirements describing how WatchKeeper was to operate and how users were to interact with WatchKeeper prior to its design and development contributed to its failed operational testing and subsequent deployment of the initial IOC project segment as the Technology Demonstrator, and ultimately, to deploying a system that does not fully meet user needs.[41]

Second, the Coast Guard did not sufficiently prioritize requirements to ensure that requirements most critical to stakeholders and users are addressed early and overall user needs are satisfied. According to project officials, they grouped WatchKeeper requirements into 17 categories that reflect similar functionality and placed each of the 17 categories into one of four "buckets"—Bucket 1 ("must have" requirements), Bucket 2 ("important" requirements), Bucket 3 (no description), and Bucket 4 ("unfunded" or "unexecutable" requirements). However, while the project office has prioritized the 17 categories of requirements, the priority of individual requirements is unclear. For example, of the remaining 256 requirements, 67 (about 26 percent) have been classified as Bucket 1 and 51 (about 20 percent) as Bucket 2.[42] However, 108 (about 42

---

[40]SEI, *CMMI® for Acquisition.*

[41]The WatchKeeper Technology Demonstrator is a Technology Demonstrator 3, which is conducted in the intended operational environment and is used to support a project's production/deployment decisions.

[42]Remaining requirements are those functional requirements that project office documentation indicated are planned for Segment 2 and service pack 4. Service packs are used to enhance or upgrade the deployed Technology Demonstrator functionality.

percent) have been classified as both Bucket 1 and Bucket 2, which diminishes the benefit of prioritization. By assigning each requirement a single priority (that is, Bucket 1, 2, 3, or 4), the project office would be better able to determine the order in which business requirements should be implemented to ensure that the most critical requirements are addressed, especially given project officials stated concern about future project funding.

Third, the Coast Guard has not demonstrated adequate traceability between its business requirements (e.g., operational and functional requirements) and system requirements.[43] Traceability of requirements is tracking the requirements from the inception of the project and agreement on a specific set of business requirements to development of the lower-level system requirements, detailed design, and test cases necessary for validating the requirements. Tracing a requirement throughout the development life cycle provides evidence that the requirements are met in the developed system and ensures that the product or system will work as intended. Requirements must be traceable forward and backward through the life cycle. The Coast Guard's Requirements Generation and Management Process recognizes the importance of traceability, stating that requirements are to be traceable throughout design, development, and test to ensure that users receive the desired capabilities.[44] According to project officials, traceability is maintained in the project's Functional Requirements Document and the System Requirements Document.[45] According to this documentation, 244 of the 355 functional requirements (about 69 percent) were traceable backward to a higher-level operational requirement and 242 of 355 functional requirements (about 68 percent) were traceable forward to lower-level system requirements. However, only 181 of the 355 functional requirements (about 51 percent) were traceable backward to both a higher-level operational requirement and forward to a lower-level system requirement. Moreover, an additional 61

---

[43]Business requirements (e.g., operational and functional requirements) describe how users will interact with the system, what the system is to do, and how well it is to do it. System requirements provide the level of detail needed for system developers to design and build the system.

[44]U.S. Coast Guard, *Requirements Generation and Management Process*, Pub 7-7, ver. 1.0 (Mar. 19, 2009).

[45]Interagency Operations Centers, *Functional Requirements Document*, v. 1,1 (May 12, 2010); and Interagency Operations Centers, *Systems Requirements Document*, v 1.0 (Sept. 12, 2011).

functional requirements were traceable to a system requirement, but were not traceable to an operational requirement. This raises questions about the genesis of these 61 functional requirements, given that functional requirements should be derived from higher-level operational requirements. Without ensuring that requirements are fully traceable, including ensuring that all lower-level requirements are traceable to a higher-level business or user requirement and all higher-level business requirements are traceable to lower-level system requirements, the program office does not have a sufficient basis for knowing whether the scope of the system will satisfy user needs.

According to project officials, these requirements management limitations are due to the aggressive schedule and limited resources for developing and deploying IOCs. However, without well-defined and managed requirements, the Coast Guard runs the risk of encountering cost overruns and schedule delays, and deploying a system with limited functionality and that does not meet user mission needs, as was the case with WatchKeeper.

Coast Guard Has Not Developed a Reliable IOC Project Cost Estimate

According to relevant guidance, a reliable cost estimate is critical to successfully delivering major information technology systems as well as major system increments such as IOC Segments 1 and 2.[46] A reliable cost estimate provides the basis for informed investment decision making, realistic budget formulation, meaningful progress measurement, and accountability for results. Our *Cost Estimating and Assessment Guide* identified four characteristics of a high-quality, reliable cost estimate: comprehensive, well-documented, accurate, and credible.

The estimated life-cycle cost estimate, dated June 2010, for the IOC project is approximately $1.6 billion. To be reliable, the cost estimate should possess all four characteristics, each of which is summarized below. The IOC cost estimate is not reliable because it does not fully satisfy the four characteristics of a reliable estimate. Specifically:

- **The estimate is not comprehensive.** To be comprehensive, the cost estimate should include a work breakdown structure (WBS) that defines the detailed work that must be accomplished to develop the

---

[46]GAO-09-3SP.

project and include all government and contractor costs over the project's life cycle—program inception through design, development, deployment, and operation and maintenance to retirement. It should also reflect all cost-influencing ground rules and assumptions and provide sufficient detail to ensure that cost elements are neither omitted nor double counted.

The IOC project does not have a comprehensive project WBS that defines all the detailed work activities needed to accomplish the project's objectives. In addition, project officials provided documentation that shows the use of at least four different WBSs, each of which is inconsistent with one another. Moreover, the Coast Guard does not have any documentation that outlines the activities that need to be completed by its development organization. Without this documentation, it will be difficult for the project office to determine if the development organization is able to deliver the desired product or if that product will meet the Coast Guard's needs. This raises questions about whether all necessary activities to accomplish the IOC's objectives have been captured, and are reflected in the cost estimate. Additionally, the cost estimate identifies costs associated with the acquisition, construction, and maintenance of the IOC project as well as contractor-related costs, but it does not include all government costs, such as those related to systems engineering and program management. Project officials said that they should have included these costs in the estimate and said that they will include them in any life-cycle cost updates. In addition, the estimate includes many, but not all, of the general assumptions that were used in the development of the cost estimate. For example, it does not discuss any potential cost limitations associated with the IOC project, participating agency support, and government-furnished equipment. Moreover, there are critical differences in the assumptions presented in the cost estimate and those presented in the independent cost estimate (as discussed later in this section). For example, the cost estimate assumes a different refresh cycle for different system hardware components, such as cameras and radars; whereas the independent estimate assumes the same refresh cycle for all hardware.

- **The estimate is not well-documented.** To be well-documented, the cost estimate should state the purpose of the estimate; provide program background, including a system description; specify the scope of the estimate (in terms of time and what is and is not included); and describe the estimating methodology and rationale. Further, management should be briefed on how the estimate was developed and provide its approval of the estimate obtained in order for the estimate to be considered valid.

The IOC project cost estimate includes the purpose, description, and scope of the project. However, it does not adequately describe the estimating methodology and rationale used to document the cost estimate. In particular, the estimate does not include information about how the specific cost elements are defined, and many of the cost elements do not include key details, such as calculations used to develop the estimate, links to the input data, or identification of cost drivers. Further, the estimate did not document contingency reserves and the associated confidence level for a risk-adjusted cost estimate.[47]

- **The cost estimate is not accurate.** To be accurate, the cost estimate should be timely and updated to reflect changes in technical or program assumptions and new phases or milestones. In addition, steps should be taken to ground the estimate in documented assumptions that can be verified by supporting data and a historical record of actual cost and schedule experiences on comparable programs. Further, the estimate should be adjusted properly for inflation.

The IOC project cost estimate has not been updated to reflect material project changes since the estimate was developed and approved. For example, the estimate does not reflect the decision to not fund Segments 3 and 4. In December 2010 and again in January 2011, DHS management directed the project office to revise the cost estimate to reflect the reduced set of requirements and to support the costs included in the Acquisition Program Baseline.[48] As noted below, project officials stated that the estimate has not been revised due to the lack of project resources. Further, the quality of key data is limited. Instead of relying on historical costs from similar projects, the estimate was based, in part, on the knowledge of subject-matter experts. In

---

[47]A risk-adjusted cost estimate has additional funding for unexpected costs added to the estimate (called management reserve) that covers expected costs above those projected by the contractor and unexpected costs in solving problems. It provides more-realistic expectations because risks have been examined and quantified and the resulting information provides probabilities associated with achieving various cost levels.

[48]The Acquisition Program Baseline summarizes the project's cost, schedule, and performance parameters, expressed in measurable, quantitative terms that must be met in order to accomplish the project's goals.

addition, the estimate specifies the inflation table used in developing the estimate, but it does not include the actual inflation numbers.

- **The estimate is not credible.** To be credible, the cost estimate should discuss any limitations in the analysis due to uncertainty or biases surrounding the data and assumptions. Major assumptions should be varied and other outcomes computed by conducting a sensitivity analysis to determine how sensitive the estimate is to changes in the assumptions. Risk and uncertainty inherent in the estimate should be assessed and disclosed including ensuring the estimate has been risk-adjusted. An independent cost estimate should also be developed to determine if other estimating methods produce similar results.

  The IOC project cost estimate was not informed by the results of a sensitivity analysis of the key cost drivers. According to the estimate, a risk and uncertainty analysis was completed. On the basis of this analysis, the current life-cycle cost estimate has approximately a 40 percent chance of being met. However, the estimate does not include the associated confidence level for a risk-adjusted cost estimate and related contingency funds. An independent cost estimate was completed for the IOC project, which was about $200 million more than the cost estimate. However, project officials were unable to explain how the differences in the two cost estimates were reconciled.

In September 2010, the project office developed an Acquisition Program Baseline for the IOC project, which focuses on a reduced set of requirements and includes a revised cost figure to acquire, develop, and deploy WatchKeeper Segments 1 and 2. According to the baseline, the acquisition costs for Segment 2 were derived using a "design to cost" strategy due to out-year budget constraints, and changes were made to the cost estimate assumptions that resulted in reduced sustainment costs for both segments. Project officials stated that the Acquisition Program Baseline costs are grounded in the information presented in the life-cycle cost estimate. However, the baseline does not identify the specific assumptions that were changed, and project officials could not provide any documentation of the assumptions used to develop the estimate. Therefore, given the weaknesses in the IOC cost estimate identified above and the absence of documented assumptions for the Acquisition Program Baseline, the reliability of the baseline cost estimate is undetermined. Project officials said that the IOC project cost estimate is not accurate and needs to be updated, and that those updates would also be made to the baseline; however project officials did not have any time frame for updating the estimate. Project officials attributed the limitations in the cost estimate to a lack of project resources and competing priorities. However, without a reliable cost estimate, the Coast Guard does not possess complete information on which to base informed investment decision making, understand system affordability, and develop justifiable budget requests.

Coast Guard Has Not Developed a Reliable IOC Project Schedule

The success of an acquisition program depends in part on having a reliable schedule of when the project's set of work activities and milestone events will occur, how long they will take, and how they are related to one another. According to GAO's *Cost Estimating and Assessment Guide,* for a schedule to be considered reliable it should, at a minimum, be

- comprehensive, with logically sequenced activities spanning the scope of work to be performed so that the full picture is available to managers;

- controlled, with a documented process for changes to the schedule so that the integrity of the schedule is assured; and

- current, with the progress on ongoing activities updated regularly so that managers can readily know the status of the project.[49]

The May 2011 integrated master schedule, which was the most current version available for our review, is not reliable because it does not fully satisfy any of the three characteristics. Examples of how these practices were and were not met are provided below.

- **Comprehensive.** As previously stated, the IOC project officials have not developed a comprehensive work breakdown structure (WBS), which would provide all activities that need to be performed in order for the project to meet its objectives. Further, the schedule does not include key efforts associated with Segment 1 system-engineering activities including the development and delivery of the first two service packs, and Segment 2 deployment activities including training.[50] Also, the schedule does not include logically sequenced activities. Specifically, of the 140 activities that remain to be

---

[49]GAO-09-3SP.

[50]Service packs are used to enhance or upgrade the deployed Technology Demonstrator functionality.

completed, 115 (about 82 percent) are not linked with associated activities. Without these linkages, activities that slip early in the schedule do not transmit delays to activities that should depend on them, and a critical path cannot be determined, which means that management is unable to determine how a slip in the completion date of a particular task may affect the overall project schedule.[51] Also, 52 of the 140 activities (37 percent) are constrained so that they cannot begin earlier than scheduled, even if previous work has been completed ahead of schedule. Additionally, of the 140 remaining activities, only 40 have resources attached to them, making it difficult for management to make appropriate decisions regarding project resources (e.g., reallocating resources).

- **Controlled**. The project office has not implemented a change-control process that preserves a baseline of the schedule so that progress can be meaningfully measured. Project officials said that the IOC project schedule has not been baselined. Nonetheless, they stated that they follow the configuration-management process as documented in the February 2010 IOC Configuration Management Plan when there are significant delays or when additional work activities are added to the schedule. These officials also stated that the configuration control board is notified of smaller date changes or delays, and noted that the IOC Project Manager chairs the control board. While these efforts may provide some insight into schedule changes, if the schedule is not appropriately baselined, project officials do not have an adequate basis upon which to measure the project's progress.

- **Current**. The project office does not have a documented process for maintaining the schedule. Project officials stated that the schedule is maintained by the IOC project team and reviewed at the biweekly Information Management Integrated Project Team (IM IPT) meetings.[52] According to these officials, updates to the schedule are done manually based on information received either verbally or by e-mail from the development organizations (i.e., Command, Control,

---

[51]The critical path represents the chain of dependent activities with the longest total duration in the schedule. If any activity on the critical path slips, the entire project will be delayed.

[52]According to the IM IPT Charter, the integrated project team is responsible for, among other things, monitoring the IOC project's cost and schedule and reporting associated risks to the Project Management Integrated Project Team.

GAO-12-202 Maritime Domain Awareness

and Communications Engineering Center and the Operations Support Center). However, project officials stated that they do not have any information about the quality of the development organizations' schedules upon which they depend to update the overall project schedule, noting that they do not know whether the activities in these schedules are properly linked. Without this information, the project office does not have assurance that the data they are using to update the schedule are reliable, and as noted above, is not in a position to determine the effect of any schedule slippage on the overall schedule.

Project officials said that reasons for the schedule weaknesses include the lack of documented processes and appropriate resources, including knowledge of scheduling practices, for developing and maintaining the schedule. Without a reliable schedule that includes all activities necessary to complete Segments 1 and 2 of the IOC project, the Coast Guard cannot accurately determine the amount of time required to complete these segments. Moreover, the Coast Guard does not have a basis for guiding the project's execution and measuring progress, thus reducing the likelihood of meeting the project's completion dates.

Collectively, the weaknesses identified with the project's integrated master schedule increase the risk of schedule slippages and related cost overruns and make meaningful measurement and oversight of project status and progress, as well as accountability for results, difficult to achieve. In the case of the IOC project, this risk has been realized. For example, according to the October 2009 IOC Project Management Plan, Segment 1 was to be deployed to all 35 sectors by March 2011 and Segment 2 by December 2015. According to the Acquisition Program Baseline, which was approved by DHS in September 2011, Segment 1 is now to be deployed to 17 of the 35 sectors by June 2012, and to the remaining 18 sectors and Segment 2 to all 35 sectors by March 2017. Moreover, the IOC project manager told us that the project has continued to experience schedule delays. According to the IOC project manager, the Coast Guard is developing a systematic approach for developing and maintaining the IOC project integrated master schedule. By developing an integrated master schedule for delivering WatchKeeper that addresses the key schedule estimating practices, the Coast Guard will be better positioned to remain on schedule and on budget as well as achieve accountability for results.

Conclusions

The Coast Guard is continuing its efforts to establish IOCs at 35 locations designed to meet the SAFE Port Act IOC requirement and share MDA information with its port partners. However, there are three factors that jeopardize such centers meeting their purpose to improve information sharing and enhance MDA across federal, state, and local port partners.

- The first factor is delays and a lack of interagency participation in developing the IOC concept. While we found that the Coast Guard has recently worked to better define IOCs and track their implementation at their sectors, the agency still faces challenges in getting other port partners to participate. Since DHS has recently become formally involved to improve interagency participation in IOCs, we are not making any recommendations relative to this issue. But we believe it is too early to tell if such recent efforts will be successful in making sure that the IOCs serve as more than Coast Guard–centric command and control centers.

- The second factor is that most port partners are not logging on to WatchKeeper—the information-sharing tool designed to assist coordination between the Coast Guard and its port partners. While we have seen some recent efforts by the Coast Guard to learn more about its port partners' needs, most occurred after the initial rollout of the WatchKeeper system. Yet recently, the Coast Guard has ended its effort to learn the extent of WatchKeeper usage by port partners and has not determined whether it wants to collect such information in the future. Without the knowledge of how successful it is in promoting port-partner usage of WatchKeeper, the Coast Guard will not be able to determine whether WatchKeeper is facilitating the IOC program in meetings its goals. Additionally, without a documented process that describes how the Coast Guard will obtain and incorporate port-partner feedback into the development of future WatchKeeper requirements in place and implemented, the Coast Guard risks deploying a system that lacks needed capabilities and, thus, limits port partners' ability to share information and coordinate in the maritime environment.

- The third factor is weak management of the IOC acquisition project, which increases the program's exposure to risk. In particular, fundamental requirements-development and management practices have not been employed; costs are unclear; and the project's schedule, which is to guide program execution and promote accountability, has not been reliably derived. By implementing key requirements-development and management practices, revising the life-cycle cost estimate for delivering WatchKeeper capabilities, and developing an integrated master schedule that addresses the key schedule-estimating practices, the Coast Guard could reduce the risk that WatchKeeper will cost more to develop and deploy than necessary. Moreover, the Coast Guard could reduce the risk that it will have a system that does not meet Coast Guard and port-partner user needs and expectations.

Without improvements in the involvement of other federal, state and local agencies, the use of WatchKeeper by port partners, and the management of the acquisition, the Coast Guard may not achieve its goals of interagency maritime integration and cooperation, and the IOCs and WatchKeeper might only serve the Coast Guard as opposed to the interagency concept intended by Congress.

Recommendations for Executive Action

To help ensure effective implementation of WatchKeeper and maximize its use among port partners, we recommend that the Commandant of the Coast Guard direct the IOC Project Manager to take the following two actions:

- collect data to determine the extent to which (1) sectors are providing port partners WatchKeeper access and (2) port partners are using WatchKeeper; and

- develop, document, and implement a process to obtain and incorporate port-partner input into the development of future WatchKeeper requirements.

To address the risks facing the Coast Guard in its acquisition and deployment of WatchKeeper, we recommend that the Commandant of the Coast Guard direct the IOC Project Manager to take the following three actions:

- implement key requirements-development and management practices to include

  (1) defining and documenting requirements, including eliciting user needs from all relevant port partners, before initiating key design activities, (2) prioritizing remaining requirements to ensure critical port-partner needs are addressed, and (3) tracing bi-directionally between higher-level operational requirements and lower-level system requirements;

- revise the IOC project life-cycle cost estimate for delivering WatchKeeper capabilities to reflect the four characteristics of a reliable estimate discussed in this report; and

- develop an integrated master schedule for delivering WatchKeeper that addresses, at a minimum, the key schedule-estimating practices discussed in this report.

Agency Comments and Our Evaluation

We provided draft copies of this report to the Secretaries of Homeland Security, Defense, and the Attorney General for review and comments. The Departments of Defense and Justice did not provide official written comments to include in the report. DHS provided official written comments, which are reprinted in appendix III. In response to our first recommendation DHS concurred and stated that the Coast Guard office responsible for IOC requirements will provide reporting parameters for the WatchKeeper system administrator to collect and report. In response to our second recommendation DHS concurred and stated that the Coast Guard is conducting surveys of all users four months after WatchKeeper delivery in a port, and IOCs will also identify additional requirements to be forwarded to the IOC project manager. Regarding our third, fourth and fifth recommendations to improve the management of the IOC acquisition, DHS concurred with all three. The department noted that their concurrence was subject to the availability of funds in the President's Fiscal Year 2013 Budget. Specifically, the department noted that the Coast Guard's Capital Investment Plan of acquisition priorities was subject to change due to a number of factors. DHS stated that it will continue to evaluate acquisition priorities in the context of, among other things, Coast Guard mission needs. In addition, DHS provided technical comments, which we incorporated as appropriate.

We are sending copies of this report to the Secretaries of Homeland Security and Defense, and the Attorney General; and interested congressional committees as appropriate. In addition, the report is available at no charge on the GAO website at http://www.gao.gov.

If you or your staff have any questions about this report, please contact me at (202) 512-9610 or caldwells@gao.gov. Contact points for our Offices of Congressional Relations and Public Affairs may be found on the last page of this report. GAO staff who made key contributions to this report are listed in appendix IV.

Stephen L. Caldwell
Director, Homeland Security and Justice Issues

List of Requesters

The Honorable John D. Rockefeller IV
Chairman
Committee on Commerce, Science, and Transportation
United States Senate

The Honorable Susan M. Collins
Ranking Member
Committee on Homeland Security and Governmental Affairs
United States Senate

The Honorable John L. Mica
Chairman
Committee on Transportation and Infrastructure
House of Representatives

The Honorable Frank A. LoBiondo
Chairman
Subcommittee on Coast Guard and Maritime Transportation
Committee on Transportation and Infrastructure
House of Representatives

The Honorable Candice S. Miller
Chairwoman
Subcommittee on Border and Maritime Security
Committee on Homeland Security
House of Representatives

The Honorable Don Young
House of Representatives

Appendix I: GAO Interviews with Port Partners

This appendix provides further details on the port partners we interviewed at the Coast Guard sectors we visited as part of the field work for the second objective (see table 2).

Table 2: GAO Interviews of Port Partners with Access to WatchKeeper

Sector	Agency/organization	Type of interview and number of port partners interviewed	Total port partners interviewed
Charleston, South Carolina	U.S. Customs and Border Protection (CBP), Office of Field Operations (OFO)	Individual (6)	
		Focus group (3)	9
	Federal Motor Carrier Safety Administration	Individual (1)	1
	U.S. Army	Individual (1)	1
	Charleston County Sheriff's Office Marine Patrol	Individual (2)	2
Total			**13**
Jacksonville, Florida	CBP OFO[a]	Individual (1)[b]	
		Focus group (4)	5
Total			**5**
Hampton Roads, Virginia	Joint Terrorism Task Force	Individual (2)	2
	Federal Bureau of Investigation (FBI)	Focus group (2)	2
	CBP OFO	Individual (4)	
		Focus group (1)	5
	U.S. Immigration and Customs Enforcement	Individual (1)	1
	Virginia Port Authority	Individual (1)	1
	City of Norfolk Harbor Patrol Unit	Focus group (1)	1
	Virginia Marine Resources Commission	Focus group (1)	1
Total			**13**
Detroit, Michigan	CBP OFO	Individual (5)	5
	CBP, Border Patrol	Individual (1)	1
	St. Clair County Office of Homeland Security/Emergency Management	Focus group (2)	2
Total			**8**
Total port partners interviewed			**39**

Source: GAO.

[a]At the time of our visit to Sector Jacksonville, CBP was the only agency to which the Coast Guard had granted access to WatchKeeper.
[b]At the time of our visit, one port partner had accessed WatchKeeper.

Appendix II: Reasons Why Port Partners Are and Are Not Using WatchKeeper

This appendix provides port partners' views on why they are and are not using WatchKeeper. Port partners we interviewed expressed mixed views on the usefulness of WatchKeeper.[1] We spoke with 17 port partners who provided us with a variety of reasons for why they are using WatchKeeper:

- 8 port partners stated they use WatchKeeper to obtain information on vessels (e.g., which port a vessel is coming from or arriving at) to perform their own missions;

- 8 port partners stated they use WatchKeeper features (e.g., Geographic Information System [GIS][2]) to perform their own missions;

- 5 port partners use WatchKeeper as a tool to facilitate coordination with the Coast Guard during vessel targeting meetings;

- 3 port partners use WatchKeeper's GIS to perform joint operations with the Coast Guard; and

- 2 port partners use WatchKeeper to perform tasks assigned to them by the Coast Guard.[3]

Twenty one port partners[4] provided us with a variety of reasons as to why they are not using WatchKeeper, and we summarized their responses into seven categories:

- 7 port partners stated WatchKeeper doesn't help them perform their own missions;

---

[1]A total of 39 port partners with access to WatchKeeper at four sectors agreed to participate in interviews and focus groups with us. See app. I for a list of the port partners we interviewed.

[2]GIS displays a ship's locations based on its automatic identification system, which is a maritime digital communication system that continually transmits and receives vessel data over very-high frequencies to identify and track vessels.

[3]Some port partners provided multiple reasons they are using WatchKeeper, therefore the number of port partners associated with the reasons does not add to 17.

[4]A total of 22 port partners we interviewed are not using WatchKeeper. One port partner did not provide a reason why not.

- 5 port partners stated they are able to obtain and share information with Coast Guard officials in-person;

- 5 port partners stated they are not able to access all features of WatchKeeper because of a firewall;

- 3 port partners stated they do not want to spend time transferring information (double entry) from their agencies own systems into WatchKeeper;

- 2 port partners stated they are unable to use WatchKeeper in the classified space in which they work;

- 2 port partners stated they are too busy to log on; and

- 1 port partner stated that WatchKeeper information is available through other systems (e.g., the Coast Guard's Ship Arrival Notification System provides information on arriving vessels).[5]

---

[5]Some port partners provided multiple reasons they are not using WatchKeeper, therefore the number of port partners associated with the reasons does not add to 21.

Appendix III: Comments from the Department of Homeland Security

U.S. Department of Homeland Security
Washington, D.C. 20528

Homeland Security

January 27, 2012

Stephen L. Caldwell
Director, Homeland Security and Justice Issues
U.S. Government Accountability Office
441 G Street, NW
Washington, DC 20548

Re: Draft Report GAO-12-202, "MARITIME SECURITY: Coast Guard Needs to Improve Use and Management of Interagency Operations Centers"

Dear Mr. Caldwell:

Thank you for the opportunity to review and comment on this draft report. The U.S. Department of Homeland Security (DHS) appreciates the U.S. Government Accountability Office's (GAO's) work in planning and conducting its review and issuing this report.

The Coast Guard, a DHS component, is responsible for establishing Interagency Operations Centers (IOCs) in response to provisions of the Security and Accountability For Every (SAFE) Port Act of 2006. IOCs are designed to, among other things, share maritime information with the Coast Guard's port partners (other agencies and organizations it coordinates with). To facilitate IOCs, the Coast Guard is implementing an information management and sharing system - WatchKeeper.

The draft report contained five recommendations which the Department concurs. Specifically, GAO recommended that the Commandant of the Coast Guard direct the IOC Project Manager to:

Recommendation 1: Collect data to determine the extent to which (1) sectors are providing port partners WatchKeeper access and (2) port partners are using WatchKeeper.

Response: Concur. The Coast Guard requirements office (CG-741) will provide reporting parameters to the Project Manager (CG-9333) for the WatchKeeper System administrator (or designated authority) to collect and report.

Recommendation 2: Develop, document, and implement a process to obtain and incorporate port partner input into the development of future WatchKeeper requirements.

Response: Concur. The Coast Guard is conducting formal user surveys of all WatchKeeper users four months after delivery of WatchKeeper to the port, the results of which will be included in development of future WatchKeeper requirements; IOCs will also collaboratively identify additional system requirements of their multi-agency members and submit requests to Project Manager. The current Configuration Control Board process enables port partners' to requests/suggestions for improvements and reports of defects to be included in service pack upgrades.

Recommendation 3: Implement key requirements development and management practices to include: (1) defining and documenting requirements, including eliciting user needs from all relevant port partners, before initiating key design activities, (2) prioritizing remaining requirements to ensure critical port partner needs are addressed, and (3) tracing bi-directionally between higher-level operational requirements and lower-level system requirements.

Response: Concur. However, the Capital Investment Plan projects Coast Guard's acquisition priorities for the next five years assuming the limits of budgetary growth set by the Budget Control Act of 2011. It does not reflect the impact of the Department of Defense's Strategy, Sustaining Global Leadership: Priorities for 21st Century Defense, which may affect operational planning at DHS. DHS will continue to evaluate Departmental acquisition priorities in the context of Homeland Security and National Security policies, including Coast Guard's statutory missions defined under 14 U.S. Code § 1, 2, 89 and 141.

Recommendation 4: Revise the IOC project life cycle cost estimate for delivering WatchKeeper capabilities to reflect the four characteristics of a reliable estimate discussed in this report.

Response: Concur. However, the Capital Investment Plan projects Coast Guard's acquisition priorities for the next five years assuming the limits of budgetary growth set by the Budget Control Act of 2011. It does not reflect the impact of the Department of Defense's Strategy, Sustaining Global Leadership: Priorities for 21st Century Defense, which may affect operational planning at DHS. DHS will continue to evaluate Departmental acquisition priorities in the context of Homeland Security and National Security policies, including Coast Guard's statutory missions defined under 14 U.S. Code § 1, 2, 89 and 141.

Recommendation 5: Develop an integrated master schedule for delivering WatchKeeper that addresses, at a minimum, the key schedule estimating practices discussed in this report.

Response: Concur. However, the Capital Investment Plan projects Coast Guard's acquisition priorities for the next five years assuming the limits of budgetary growth set by the Budget Control Act of 2011. It does not reflect the impact of the Department of Defense's Strategy, Sustaining Global Leadership: Priorities for 21st Century Defense, which may affect operational planning at DHS. DHS will continue to evaluate Departmental acquisition priorities in the context of Homeland Security and National Security policies, including Coast Guard's statutory missions defined under 14 U.S. Code § 1, 2, 89 and 141.

2

Again, thank you for the opportunity to review and comment on this draft report. Technical comments were previously provided under separate cover. We look forward to working with you on future Homeland Security issues.

Sincerely,

Jim H. Crumpacker
Director
Departmental GAO-OIG Liaison Office

3

Appendix IV: GAO Contact and Staff Acknowledgments

GAO Contact	Stephen L. Caldwell, (202) 512-9610 or caldwells@gao.gov
Staff Acknowledgments	In addition to the contact named above, Christopher Conrad and Deborah Davis, Assistant Directors, and Jonathan Bachman, Analyst-in-Charge, managed this review. Lisa Canini, Mary Fike, Nicholas Jepson, and Karl Seifert made significant contributions to the work. In addition, David Powner and Timothy Persons provided technical assistance with information-technology issues; Michele Fejfar and Steven Putansu assisted with design and methodology; Karen Richey and Tisha Derricotte assisted with cost-estimating and scheduling analysis; Geoffrey Hamilton provided legal support; Jessica Orr and Lara Miklozek provided assistance in report preparation; and Muriel Brown and Joshua Ormond developed the report's graphics.

Related GAO Products

Homeland Defense: Actions Needed to Improve DOD Planning and Coordination for Maritime Operations. GAO-11-661. Washington, D.C.: June 23, 2011.

Coast Guard: Opportunities Exist to Further Improve Acquisition Management Capabilities. GAO-11-480. Washington, D.C.: April 13, 2011.

Maritime Security: Federal Agencies Have Taken Actions to Address Risks Posed by Seafarers, but Efforts Can Be Strengthened. GAO-11-195. Washington, D.C.: January 14, 2011.

Border Security: Enhanced DHS Oversight and Assessment of Interagency Coordination Is Needed for the Northern Border. GAO-11-97. Washington, D.C.: December 17, 2010.

Information Sharing: DHS Could Better Define How It Plans to Meet Its State and Local Mission and Improve Performance Accountability. GAO-11-223. Washington, D.C.: December 16, 2010.

Maritime Security: Ferry Security Measures Have Been Implemented, but Evaluating Existing Studies Could Further Enhance Security. GAO-11-207. Washington, D.C.: December 3, 2010.

Maritime Security: Responses to Questions for the Record. GAO-11-140R. Washington, D.C.: October 22, 2010.

Maritime Security: DHS Progress and Challenges in Key Areas of Port Security. GAO-10-940T. Washington, D.C.: July 21, 2010.

Department of Homeland Security: Assessments of Selected Complex Acquisitions. GAO-10-588SP. Washington, D.C.: June 30, 2010.

Maritime Security: Varied Actions Taken to Enhance Cruise Ship Security, but Some Concerns Remain. GAO-10-400. Washington, D.C.: April 9, 2010.

Information Sharing: Federal Agencies Are Sharing Border and Terrorism Information with Local and Tribal Law Enforcement Agencies, but Additional Efforts Are Needed. GAO-10-41. Washington, D.C.: December 18, 2009.

Maritime Security: Vessel Tracking Systems Provide Key Information, but the Need for Duplicate Data Should Be Reviewed. GAO-09-337. Washington, D.C.: March 17, 2009.

Maritime Security: National Strategy and Supporting Plans Were Generally Well-Developed and Are Being Implemented. GAO-08-672. Washington, D.C.: June 20, 2008.

Maritime Security: The SAFE Port Act: Status and Implementation One Year Later. GAO-08-126T. Washington, D.C.: October 30, 2007.

Maritime Security: The SAFE Port Act and Efforts to Secure Our Nation's Seaports. GAO-08-86T. Washington, D.C.: October 4, 2007.

GAO's Mission	The Government Accountability Office, the audit, evaluation, and investigative arm of Congress, exists to support Congress in meeting its constitutional responsibilities and to help improve the performance and accountability of the federal government for the American people. GAO examines the use of public funds; evaluates federal programs and policies; and provides analyses, recommendations, and other assistance to help Congress make informed oversight, policy, and funding decisions. GAO's commitment to good government is reflected in its core values of accountability, integrity, and reliability.
Obtaining Copies of GAO Reports and Testimony	The fastest and easiest way to obtain copies of GAO documents at no cost is through GAO's website (www.gao.gov). Each weekday afternoon, GAO posts on its website newly released reports, testimony, and correspondence. To have GAO e-mail you a list of newly posted products, go to www.gao.gov and select "E-mail Updates."
Order by Phone	The price of each GAO publication reflects GAO's actual cost of production and distribution and depends on the number of pages in the publication and whether the publication is printed in color or black and white. Pricing and ordering information is posted on GAO's website, http://www.gao.gov/ordering.htm. Place orders by calling (202) 512-6000, toll free (866) 801-7077, or TDD (202) 512-2537. Orders may be paid for using American Express, Discover Card, MasterCard, Visa, check, or money order. Call for additional information.
Connect with GAO	Connect with GAO on Facebook, Flickr, Twitter, and YouTube. Subscribe to our RSS Feeds or E-mail Updates. Listen to our Podcasts. Visit GAO on the web at www.gao.gov.
To Report Fraud, Waste, and Abuse in Federal Programs	Contact: Website: www.gao.gov/fraudnet/fraudnet.htm E-mail: fraudnet@gao.gov Automated answering system: (800) 424-5454 or (202) 512-7470
Congressional Relations	Katherine Siggerud, Managing Director, siggerudk@gao.gov, (202) 512-4400, U.S. Government Accountability Office, 441 G Street NW, Room 7125, Washington, DC 20548
Public Affairs	Chuck Young, Managing Director, youngc1@gao.gov, (202) 512-4800 U.S. Government Accountability Office, 441 G Street NW, Room 7149 Washington, DC 20548

Please Print on Recycled Paper.